As a child
my eyes
heard it first

Timothy G. Green

As a child my eyes heard it first

2nd Edition

Copyright © 2019 by Timothy G. Green

ISBN 978-1-949402-06-3 (Paperback Black & White)
ISBN 978-1-949402-09-4 (Paperback Color)
ISBN 978-1-949402-10-0 (Hardcover Color)

Editor: Mary Mitchell - marymitchell139@yahoo.com

Cover Design: Donna Osborn Clark at CreationsByDonna@gmail.com

Layout and Interior Design: Creative Unity Productions

Published by: **INKaissance Books**
inkaissance@gmail.com

INKaissance Books

On January 15, 1978, a child who was deemed as being detrimental to his own mothers' health was brought into this world. This child's mother had severe internal complications which prompted doctors to assess that not only was there a chance that she would lose her child but there was a high possibility that she would injure herself as well upon giving birth.

Being the loving, devoted and faithful mother she was she refused to mentally give in and instead she turned to console in the Lord. By her selfless act of courage and faith Timothy G. Green entered into this world.

Ephesians 6:2-3 New Living Translation

[2] "Honor your father and mother." This is the first commandment with a promise: [3] If you honor your father and mother, "things will go well for you, and you will have a long life on the earth."

The jewel of a Ruby

Silence is of her nature yet

her speech is as sweet as nectar,

that is why I have sworn, on behalf of my soul,

to always protect her,

especially when I express my love for her

via display at public lectures,

I'm sure to acknowledge the pureness

of her soul's texture...

Even through my very first letter written

to her – instantly I felt her energy,

for she inspired my words to glide soulfully like

the balance of an orchestrated symphony,

Richly, I fell in love with her heart for I realized

"special" was this gift she sent to me,

for unlike many women in my life,

she entertained my heart differently,

Ever so gentle, with maturity and utmost adoration…

Allowing me to vent not only to but through her,

vowing to never show resentment,

for when I write or even recite she looks me in the soul

with a calm control - so attentive,

In retrospect she has already
ordained me as gifted!

She has always been sincere to purpose in my life
never acting out to gain false attention,
pouring God's love and prayer in to me consistently
as a true woman of honor and angelic distinction,
she's the first earthly love of my life
and inspires me to continue living,
in her precious name; Ruby,
symbolically poetry!

My mother… I love you with the entire God in me!

Table of Contents

Preface

Psalm 34:19 New Living Translation
"The righteous person faces many troubles,
but the Lord comes to the rescue each time."

Ashes, Ashes, we all fall down

Perfected poignant waterfalls release from my eyes
as I hear the cries of the hungered fetus who thirsts life
yet, abortion is set to spell his untimely & unfortunate demise...
Undeveloped are his arms yet they stretch
towards the surface of the womb,
reaching for freedom & his mother's comfort
not knowing her inner will embodies his soul as a tomb...

YOUR TORCH SHALL BURN ON

So beautiful and innocent with a smile sculpted so heavenly
not knowing the imperfections of your childhood
are in grave jeopardy
you dislike the touch of daddy and as your heart
seeks refuge desperately...
His kisses are vicious - damned broken promises fictitious

reflections of being a man distorted
like shattered fragments of cracked dishes
his lustful ways overshadow the hope of flamed
birthday candles and their wishes
the more he pushes, you show restraint,
yet the bastard keeps pushing...

YOUR TORCH SHALL BURN ON

Mommy & Daddy abuse you, inflicting anguish
upon your flesh
as your bones weaken my soul mournfully begins speaking
to Mother Nature, may she nurture your body
with purified milk from her breast
may Father Time erode the conscience of your parents ensuring
in peace they never rest
as guilt shall imprint its affliction within
their minds and burn dismay in its nest
punishing them to damnation...
a warrant of justice for this civil arrest

YOUR TORCH SHALL BURN ON

Underfed and succumbing to malnutrition
the sight of a child starving
I too ask, "What's going on?" In retrospect to

the gifted brother Marvin

I felt your spirits uplifting as I served you meals

at the local soup kitchen...

My heart freely wept as it attempted to trace

your struggles every step...

The homeless children of the world shall forever

remain close to me

for my undying & unconditional love are a free buffet to them

to feast upon at will and to serve as infinite groceries

YOUR TORCH SHALL BURN ON...

As A Child My Eyes Heard It First

Isaiah 54:17 New Living Translation

"But in that coming day

no weapon turned against you will succeed.

You will silence every voice

raised up to accuse you.

These benefits are enjoyed by the servants of the Lord;

their vindication will come from me.

I, the Lord, have spoken!"

P.A.I.N.

Poverty, Agony, Ignorance, Neglect

On park benches, within our playground,

thugs slang drugs and syringes

acting as generals and soldiers while scheming

and plotting actions of vengeance

their eyes would glaze as they would get high

sparking blunts like incense

scenery so intense that as children we

watched from a close distance.

Our souls were securely embraced by rest-in-peace murals

painted in loving care and remembrance

of tenants and unborn infants diminished

through Satan's arithmetic

many of their lives were lost from being

put in discomforting predicaments.

As a child my eyes remember hearing these sentiments

that condemned many people in society as hypocrites

for I then realized that many people sentenced life to death

without knowing their differences...

In retrospect to death it was never unusual for us

to attend a loved one's funeral

while feeling the after effects of Satan slowly burning

America the beautiful

school teachers often attempted to teach us

to think outside the box

but when in reality the ghetto appeared to form a cubicle

I mean not even the elder tenants could see the sun rising

for it was hidden too deep within the clouds

so this fear of survival remained mutual.

Especially when the cops would stroll through the hood and

scream "stand up"

and many of us who reacted slowly were served

a brutal beating after being handcuffed

as a young boy my father told me

to observe it all and man up...

My eyes heard what he said as I envisioned the many times

my mother's soul bled

by example she always led, I mean she worked two jobs

in order to keep the family fed

funny because as a child mostly all the books I read

always portrayed the man as the head...

of the household but in my neighborhood many

fathers hid in mouse holes

while single mothers wore the pants and enhanced wisdom

amongst their children

while watching their spouse fold

even alcohol had the reputation and tendency

to knock a lot of people out cold

so as a child I challenged its stature in a sense

that was seen as being ignorantly bold!

From my first taste, I reverted back to being a baby,

a new bottle I would embrace

how sweet the sound to my throat was this amazing grace...

It felt like my vision was duct-taped for many of us

who were born in this city of thieves

in which our uniformed dreams of getting

cash money easily deceived

some of us fell prey to depression and contemplated

suicide through Russian Roulette

with no regret many of us often "cocked and squeezed..."

Heavily clouded were our lungs as they would willingly

bleed from smoking ounces of weed

as youth we felt under siege so we opted to hustle

while the street war gradually intrigued

the ghetto was and still is often seen

by society as Hell's debris

resulting in childless mothers praying

to God mercilessly on bent knees.

As they cried these painful pleas their very breath

could be heard shortening in dire fatigue

a universal pain in the ghetto,

for as one unit we would all grieve

helplessly inhaling this vicious life threatening disease...

Many high school athletes from the ghetto

drew guns to script pictures

while forfeiting their desires of someday

playing in the NBA league

a process in which many of us learned to read the lines

of politicians slowly and in between.

Their motives were never to destroy

poverty but to gain monopoly

as they hoped this act of athlete recruitment

would cover up their scheme...

Rap and Hip Hop permitted us direct access

to exercise our freedom of speech

but at times we allowed Gangster rappers to distort our reality

and many of our dreams

as many of us children imitated this art and turned to the

corner to hustle cocaine

endorsing our pain to the world like victims

in horror movies who inevitably scream.

We see life as a blind man's gamble where

Aces and Spades empower Kings & Queens

so instead of cleaning up our act

we gamble dirty for we feel worthy

of meeting and greeting death amongst finer things...

We boldly listened to police sirens sing

as they headed to an everyday scene

where beneath a streetlight dwells a bleak sight -

a motionless body of a slain teen...

Maybe now one can see why many of our attitudes were

sculpted and molded

in the form of being mean.

I mean the streets have an influence on us

but at times we are our worst enemy

during my childhood years I was

overweight and prone to hate

as my peers harassed me with many verbal obscenities...

Remarks so painful, that at age 11,

regrettably I lost my virginity

I was only attempting to prove not to my peers

but to myself that I could be loved tenderly

truth be told, the uncontrolled emotions of my hormones

orchestrated this symphony

for no matter how hard I would try

I would still be looked upon differently

forever, As a child, my eyes hearing would

be scarred and damaged mentally

from exploring the wants and needs of

my heart being touched sensually.

As a child my eyes heard the guilty verdict of being judged

for I was one of many children who just wanted to be loved...

Just loved for the people we were

I mean almost every day our perilous quest

for life's answers would be deferred.

It was a group of us who met behind

the dumpsters in the projects

attempting to be taught sex 101 from playboy magazines

but sex was just too complex

so in return, for women,

most of us had a false sense of respect

especially a selected few whose mothers

were abusive drug addicts...

In conclusion, women and love didn't seem compatible,

so in their minds

a woman's purpose was solely to neglect

As a child my eyes heard the cause as my heart

strenuously felt the effect

black and white, wrong from right

a puzzling sight as nothing seemed to be consciously correct.

Even the project untouchables began

to build their own caskets

top hustlers turned snitch to avoid prison time

and hearing the guilty verdict

as if the bullets which ricocheted swift like a

switchblade choreographed it

children walking, riding bikes and roller-skating

were caught in this drug traffic

as my eyes heard some children holding and tasting

product stashes for hustlers

which eventually began the development of a habit.

More so a development of pure madness in which

the projects became infested

for many young girls played Double Dutch but so many

were troubled-touched and wrongfully molested

some by people who were sworn by

blood to keep them protected

Fathers, Brothers, and Uncles...

minds conquered by sexual poison and deeply infected.

So many times when my eyes would hear the hate

desperately I tried to escape

we didn't have basketball hoops

so we used the services of milk crates

I mean some days we played morning to night

wishing these evil realities would deflate

for this playful getaway was recognized as our fortress

unfortunately we couldn't keep outsiders out

Timothy G. Green

for we had no gates

there we learned that the ropes of survival

had many high stakes...

Adjacent to our court was an old abandoned building,

a shelter to the homeless

one time at school I asked officer Friendly

how could the police department condone this

he gave a long winded speech about

how poverty was a worldwide opponent

but this was information I already knew –

an everyday picture my project drew

so we were sworn to poverty, I could never disown it...

And we learned from these homeless people

who we once called bums

that they too were people, deemed by the

very breath that filled their lungs

sole survivors who learned to adjust in the world

without materialistic possessions

for their soul's danced to a different drum.

Engraved in their minds had to be a

willful and simplistic design to survive

which they would utilize daily

regardless of all the times society withstood them

for it seemed no matter what outcome would derive

they believed God was their protector who swore

an oath to forever protect hoodlums.

As a child my eyes could hear us

in the sandbox making hand prints

Godly seemed this gift of pure emotional innocence

just like the many Mormons and Christians

who handed out "God loves you" pamphlets.

My eyes also heard grown men

make several sexual advancements

To prostitutes who gave salutes by flashing bodily attributes.

Momma always assured us, the children,

that their actions were far from cute

instructing us to observe their actions with our eyes

but our mouths must remain mute.

However, momma said we must not

forget that they too needed prayer

so every night when she spoke to the Lord,

she spoke very sincere

holding the word of God to its highest creed,

expecting the Lord to adhere

and purify their minds and a lifestyle

she viewed as a nightmare

begging God to cleanse their souls at His will

for she was readily obedient to continue

the sacrificing of her tears.

Over the years, As a child, my eyes would hear

many of my parent's arguments

and I being young figured when two souls disagreed

a gap was bridged in their partnership

for being the youngest child I couldn't allow

my emotions to stand in denial

as I envisioned divorce being the result

of my parent's many quarrels - the final consequence.

However, through this rough endeavor Gods

grace held my family together

and brought our souls to a peaceful place

of heavenly prominence

as we believed this was a sign from God

as He again displayed his spiritual dominance.

You see, my mother began to teach us that Jesus was the truth

and proof of divine eminence

she would place her hands on our hearts

during prayer so we could feel His

humble aura and tenderness

and once we were healed His love and mercy

would be revealed

gratefully we would reap from Jesus' selfless love

and abundance of sacrificial benefits.

Often my eyes would blink as I still tasted

salty tears of negligence

and the result burned my eyes, vision which has been affected

and altered dramatically ever since...

I remember my first job, working under the table

where my employers were racist

although I was discouraged my father would not allow

me to quit - he refused

their actions to have my confidence

pummeled and literally subdued.

He and I then reflected on his work ethic

and the moral would conclude

that I would continue to work hard, be on time,

and speak respectfully - never rude

for my father believed in due time my

character would act as food

and feed my employers an uncanny

and unexpected mature minded attitude...

As a child I was taught to respect the heart

and courage my ancestors portrayed

for many were shamed and pained but

still were striving to pay their dues

thus As a child my eyes heard that Black is beautiful

and till this day it keeps my heart fueled!

But, some took it upon themselves to act crude

as my dark complexion was ridiculed

so obviously one would understand why

80% of my childhood was spent in the foulest of moods.

Dr. Martin Luther King and I share the same

birthday which reminds me of his love for the Negro

which would gradually intrude

on my depression, which I acknowledged as a blessing,

for it was a humbling interlude.

Thus, methodically my self esteem began to actually improve

I could feel my shoulders broaden and rise

parallel to the horizon

for I thought I was no longer confused

until another black man called me a "no good nigger"...

I was too young to swallow my pride so my mind

had succumb to a state of solitude.

My heartbeat suddenly was found helplessly

yearning while tossing and turning

expeditiously burning as my mind was in

dire pursuit to be soothed.

Understand that as a child I thought

I wasn't capable of handling the pressure

so I wanted all of this

"**P**overty, **A**gony, **I**gnorance, and **N**eglect"

to immediately be removed.

I felt that all of this pressure and weight on

my shoulders was unfair

for I was born into the world guilt-free and nude...

at least I thought.

As a child my eyes heard the painful cries of roaches

how their legs would scamper – when sight of a RAID can

was their ode of death approaching…

It was a natural closeness because

in the projects we're also seen as culprits

deemed by many people to be a lost generation and hopeless

their stereotypes were hatefully spiteful from what

my eyes gathered from their judgmental diagnosis...

So Saint Eyes watered our plants and we sagged our pants,

So why wouldn't we be expected to grow black roses?

We were labeled as endangered angered suspects,

with no sense of having focus

boy, were they wrong, we hustled dusk to dawn,

in order not to be the broke-est.

Behind the corner store we saw neighborhood

teachers and preachers suffering from overdoses

ungodly & melancholy is the tune P.A.I.N. often composes...

Bodies consistently boarded ambulances in two's

like the animals onto the ark with Noah

as from this world their souls would depart and embark

judgment from God, which was said to come a lot slower.

As a child my eyes remember hearing cocaine

rumble through crack addicts veins

intense like the saliva smothering a famine

stricken pit bulls chain

some would call their actions an act of shame...

But to them it was a daily ritual

the game of survival of the fittest

where the playing field was constructed to be difficult

please allow what my eyes heard as a child

to provide you with a visual.

Seeing my childhood friends driven away in squad cars

was grievous like having a slit throat...

If our life was a piano then failure would be

found as the renowned off note!

Remember, As a child my eyes heard the painful

cries of the cockroach running for safety

they also heard the ghetto screaming

"Why does God hate me…"

Even though as a child many of us were

raised in the church faithfully.

I remember how slow I would walk to the

cash register often catching cramps

my feet felt cemented, as did my soul, which felt tormented

so slowly I would advance...

Picture as a child my eyes hearing other

customers laughing at a glance

because they could visibly see my hand

firmly clutching a booklet of food stamps

my head dragged worse than the crooked double cuffs

on my oversized pants.

As time passed through my childhood years my mind

amplified into a more stalwart stance

the collaboration of food stamps and food in the frying pan

shined and dined our hunger through a magical dance.

Instantly it brightened and enlightened our souls

like fluorescent bulbs in lamps

so I questioned the man in the mirror and politely asked Him,

"Is poverty a scripted act in my life just by chance?

Looking back at the many times my friends

stole their parents' cigarettes

they didn't possess the knowledge to know that

the poison within it posed bigger threats

in unconscious distress they inhaled and consumed

a bulk of fumes with no regrets

unbalancing and not valuing their lungs

and breath as vital assets...

Rarely were we disciplined from school text

but rather from the gift and curse of experience

which always maintained a watchful eye over us

like the ancient Egyptian pyramids

at times it paced us like the wheels on baby carriages

because so many dramatic events brought forth outcomes

such as unlawful marriages

some requiring scars and wounds to be

healed by the support of bandages.

As a child my eyes heard the vivid rhythm of white chalk

outlining victims on concrete canvasses

but my family was blessed to have daddy as a

Preacher and mommy as an Evangelist

they saw us through the toughest times and secured

us as best they could

from the deepest depths of Satan's wilderness...

Ironically, a lot of thieves found fame

on surveillance cameras

supplying and delivering addicts with drugs

as if they were package handlers

my eyes remember hearing the names of familiar

gamblers on local police scanners

just as the many graphic stories of corpses being

carted away by paramedics

especially those who were caught in the

cross fire as innocent bystanders.

Damn, it seemed like death continued to display his authority

by raising his painful standards

all the while, having narcotics seduce our

mentality like exotic lap dancers

as if all this violence was a questionnaire and our parents

were in desperate search of answers

of how they could prevent us children

from being raised with vile manners...

Our mind states were so uncivil that our snotty

noses walked hand and hand with all of our ailing sniffles

because so many times we were puzzled like jigsaw,

as if our lives were unsolvable riddles.

As a child my eyes heard many grown men who were afraid

to be chosen take the stance of liberals

they smacked us fearlessly across our mouths

when they misunderstood our giggles

furiously our hearts would sizzle

on our cheeks tears would trickle

but little did our fathers know that our love for them

would never freeze like icicles...

No matter how many times they were responsible

for putting our mothers in hospitals

we were baby cubs in need of love and comfort

softer than goosed-feathered pillows

though our hearts were very brittle and viewed as being little

in the lives of mommy and daddy

we yearned to just be in the middle

the shining stars and centers of attention...

Yes, in the lives of mommy and daddy

we yearned to be just in the middle

because as children our hearts were just so very little

our hearts were very brittle

at least we knew Jesus loved the little children

for that hymn was engrained biblical...

So many times I stood as a coward and watched

from a distance

as my friends easily engaged in acts of thievery

and desperation by shoplifting

as my body perspired fearfully, I could be found outside

with my hands in my pockets whistling

scared half to death 'cause momma always said,

"In accordance to our thoughts

we should best believe that God was always listening."

From where I was positioned

I could have somehow intervened

but snitching was disloyal and dirty amongst our team

so I chose to portray loyalty & keep my trust record clean...

Even though these were the same friends

who found joy in teasing me at recess

as their feet sported Nike's while my feet wore an unknown

brand of sneakers labeled as rejects.

Already being overweight at a young age was so frustrating

that I would often be found pondering in distress

searching for outlets of acceptance from my peers

and family for my soul to caress.

I never knew how to appreciate my mental jewels which

paved the way for a lot of my youthful success

because in depth I was lacking knowledge of self and not

sure in "self" how to invest.

As a child my eyes heard a conversation

amongst a group of pigeons

and what I found to be inspiring was their blueprint

of survival and articulated vision

because they were driven to be beautiful no matter how many

people's opinions may beg to differ

for they gladly feast off of the countless dollars of food

we as a society waste through litter

for they always seemed appreciative of these handouts

and never did they act bitter.

As a child my eyes heard the similarities of their lives

and ours as I took time to consider how

these pigeons survived by all means necessary

never wanting or waiting for anyone to hand deliver.

Although there were some who feed them bread faithfully

and were blessed for being givers

despite this act of kindness there still were many nights that

these pigeons heads were rained upon

and in the cold they would helplessly shiver.

Regardless, like the pigeons they have a humble soul

that allows them to simply roll

with the flow one day at a time down life's

turbulent yet peaceful river.

Bootleggers chose to oppose working legally and opted not

to start at minimum wage

so many of them hustled music CD's and coats

made of denim and suede...

I remember the Sunday sermons where the preacher often

said we as a people were sinning with rage

As a child my eyes remember hearing how the footsteps of

these events rapidly led to us growing and coming of age.

Hanging with the older guys often meant our clothes would

have the scent of Newports

and when we would return home our parents would put us on

the stand and play the judge in their court

many times they struck fear in our hearts similar

to one being on life support

as we hoped they would have mercy and forgive

us for our mistakes

portraying the opposite of being selfish

and show us warmth...

But, there were some parents who got their

point across by exercising brutal force

using children as punching bags as if hitting

us was recreation and sport

some wounds take longer to heal than others

so today this affliction

still has the tendency to scorch

as these reflections in our minds seem to burn incessantly

with the potency of a torch.

So potent that many of us often wished instead of birth

our parents had opted to abort

because it seemed like they could not smell our potential

due to the coke they would snort

so our expectations and their dreams would readily distort.

In short, it seemed without rear view mirrors we drove

recklessly on this Hell-bound crash course

because we lacked answers to questions

of our immediate future

citing these unforgettable times as the problem,

the ultimate malevolent source.

As a child I remember hearing my friends coughing

as we played hide-n-seek

due to hallways scented like urine

where the walls were paper thin and we could

hear tenants spreading rumors

that would spin like whirlwinds and through

the projects rumor mill would start stirring.

Adding fuel to the fire was the violence that

would once again start recurring

and when the cops would question tenants as to what

was the cause of isolated incidents

90% of the time they would respond in a manner uncertain.

As a child my eyes remember hearing how this image

continued to keep the projects hurting

in terms of marketability and government funds which often

left the projects hung like curtains.

Unfortunately, we the children, the next generation,

were left to carry this burden

as newborns were destined to represent **H.O.P.E.** through life

but slowly they started to represent **P.A.I.N.** as the roles

of life and death begin reversing.

I mean homeless men and women would

sleep outside on dirty mattresses

yet be unaccounted for by the Census Bureau

as part of the world's populated masses

but they did have a purpose in the world too

like the physical laws of cigarettes

not being able to function without lighters,

stove tops, heat or matches.

As a child I remember hearing the thunder caused

by reckless drivers in car crashes

someone's life and dreams were now shattered

as if they were frameless broken glasses.

This led to our fear growing rapidly in alignment

at the pace of how time passes

many times flickering at blinding speeds

faster than our own eyelashes

This **P.A.I.N.** was overbearing at times

and today it still harasses...

I am moved by the winds differently,

I speak in gregarious tones only identified by calligraphy,

I keep my father in the forefront of my mind,

never too far in distant memory,

releasing smoke from my chest, to the sky as I cry,

like that of a chimney,

My soul is full of depression yet it often feels empty,

when I allow the rigorous sins of the world

to gradually tempt me…

I am simply a poetic voice, a scribe who is destined to write,

Satan fractures my knuckles on his accord

yet I write despite,

I walk the earth blind allowing God to guide my light,

as memoirs of my trials and tribulations

serve my soul precious insight…

I invite others freely to engage in

my life's journey & experience,

knowing that I am a project from the projects

in mankind's lab experiment,

I am far from sinless, consistently found

before the Lord in repentance,

for when my number is called I pray

it is with God's chosen,

that I shall stand in attendance...

My eyes open bloodshot, not from liquor but from dwelling in my past,

reflecting on my low esteem when I knew answers

but wouldn't raise my hand in class,

I received low grades for a while only because

I was afraid to walk on the "smart" student path,

but damn I suffered for it as my peers would harass

my lack of "shown "intelligence with degrading laughs...

As a child my eyes could hear the sickening discussions

taking place amongst pedophiles

they didn't have to utter a word yet discomfort

was felt by the sinful zest of their smiles...

A filthy look of guilt was worn on their face,

dirty like the thickness of muddy tile

as if they wanted it to be seen by all,

the sickness of a mind confused and senile.

Although blood ran through their veins it seemed

like their heartbeats were not stably vital

for any motive to be sexually controlling, towards a child,

seemed to be evil all the while...

As the cases against these child molesters begin to pile

the liveliness of their victims childhood began

to become desolate and idle.

There were rumors that two local neighborhood merchants

were a part of this pedophile inner circle and blended

in well amongst these serpents

it was said they would lure them by handing out free candy

making children feel welcome

versus dejected, rejected and worthless,

for that was the key to gaining their trust,

it was their sole purpose.

However, at one point victimized children saw a brief speck

of light as they assumed the store

had a major change in management

however the store only changed its name and the

workers remained the same inflicting

more pain ever so scandalous.

The community acknowledged this store

as an asset and couldn't afford to leave it in abandonment

for the children never told their parents

of the horrid acts going on

in an attempt to save face and embarrassment.

The tears from the eyes of these children were vividly painful,

there was no withstanding it

for if every trip to the store was set afloat on a boat

then wicked were the winds guiding the sails of this

disastrous course and steering it.

I remember in the center of our projects

when gangs would assemble for meetings

As a child my eyes could hear the agony

of future gang members screaming

during their initiation as many were agonized while brutally

taking a beating

and if they survived, hugs were exchanged and sacred

handshakes in the form of greetings.

Gangs swarmed the streets habitually

like cement on sidewalks

as anti-violence groups revolted by hosting community

rallies aimed directly at these heathens.

Gangs carried the reputation of having the sinew

of shedding blood during all seasons

researching city statistics on their growth provides evidence

of their numbers growing immensely

month by month as our cities fear began to deepen

even when the streets were restless from drug droughts

as hustlers could be heard weeping.

Still, gangs reinforced their power via

frightening displays of weaponry

which at intervals lead to the dismantling of stolen cars

and the selling of their accessories

without hesitation, put to death were those who chose

to oppose these demeanors as felonies

for many gang members killed at will

in a methodical sense so effortlessly

unfortunately, this hatred for life

seemed to bear no discrepancies.

Even the law enforcement attempted to build

neighborhood committees to assist

planning security measures to cut down

on the cities casualties.

Many of the top drug distributors in the State

were rumored to be CEO's of established faculties

whose stature was held high in society

as they looked down on the city from corporate balconies.

As a child my eyes heard many hustlers shuffling

their drugs deep inside music speakers

as others hid their currency profits evenly

creased in the soles of sneakers.

Some thugs literally acted out the name

of wearing wife beaters

as they brutally beat the women they were with;

their self proclaimed divas.

Yet, despite being abused so many women

stayed loyal to these men

although they possessed overwhelming evidence

that these men were cheaters

some were attracted to the thug persona, high profile,

expensive car driving features

but many of these men were known as gutless

cowards as they sacrificed loyalty

for their own freedom and snitched willingly

on their "so called" brother's keepers...

Making plea bargains with district attorneys had its karma

enforced directly by the grim reaper.

In this act of betrayal if they were caught

then the onslaught would be possible execution…

evident because As a child my eyes remember hearing bullets

ricocheting throughout the playground

monkey bars from rival shootings.

Former allies now plighted in warfare amongst

the tenants caused confusion

but those of us close to the situation understood

the repercussions of disloyalty

and were fully immune to this pollution.

In conclusion, not even politicians and city officials

offered a viable solution

and many of them used this violence for self advocacy

and acted as if they were giving actual

contribution to end the feuding.

However, it was their image, to obtain votes in the near

future, which they were boosting

As a child my eyes remember hearing in astonishment

this spiteful optical illusion

but regardless, in front office positions, these politicians

continued to steadily move in...

but as we grew as children we knew some things to be true

such as **H.O.P.E.** being our strongest

virtue to carry us through...

You have to understand that the heartbeat of

we the children was pure as egg yolk

for our kindred spirits out grew our age, as many residents

began to recognize us as kinfolk.

Our maturity was elevating to superior heights

evident by the confidence portrayed

through the very words we spoke

for our lives were vividly being sculpted in the midst

of the gloomiest fog smoke.

Please realize we began to learn how to balance life and death

on experiences tight rope...

Pertaining to life we discovered a new found appreciation

which served as preparation for our future

Timothy G. Green

endeavors influenced by **H.O.P.E.**

Suddenly I find myself laying face down handcuffed

with a knee daggered in my spine

racial slurs being directed at me

as if the color black can't be shined

saliva from my oppressor drips down my face

as I can hear his fellow colleagues laughing

I say, "I'll meet you in hell to settle the score"

just before my head begins to receive a brutal bashing

night sticks pound my chest like ancient tribal drums

breathing heavy - face catching a cleansing

from palms sweaty

struggling to rise from the feet of these cowards

yet my strength is faint, so I show restraint,

cars driving by with no tires screeching to halt

perhaps a teenager with his life dangling in danger

As a child my eyes heard it first

is being justified by

Poverty – Agony – Ignorance – Neglect…

jaw swollen from the size 12 that kissed it

as blood flows innocently in streams from my nostrils

the beating ceases in the wind as I hear voices retreating

keys then free my wrist rather slowly and gently

sarcastic apologies are given as I lay

nearly numb & lifeless

all due to the police departments mistaken identity

slowly I stand up, in dire **P.A.I.N.,** drenched in sweat

anger dancing on the tip of my tongue

but no words can release

derived from a punctured lung

which promised that a story of **H.O.P.E.**

would still be sung…

IN SPITE OF

H.O.P.E.

Happiness of Prayers Embracing

As a child my eyes fell in love with hearing

the melodies of ice cream trucks

as I remember rushing to my piggy bank to withdraw

coins in the amount of two bucks.

One could imagine this joyous anticipation

which had the power to measure

the speed of how fast a child's heart could truly pump

equaling the enthusiasm a young

boy expresses after receiving

his first day of school haircut.

How crisp it is when it matches the symmetric creases in his

classroom picture day tux

for riding this wave of cheerfulness was reminiscent of bath

time with rubber ducks...

How good it feels to be so overwhelmed with

joy that when danger approaches

your heart and soul avoid it as they collaboratively jump...

Looking back at my parents combined income one would

ask how did our family manage

well, we as children were thankful for

the nights at the dinner table

when the main course meal was fried bologna sandwiches

we were fortunate enough to have a meal and today

these moments our hearts still cherish.

Please understand as children we were taught to

appreciate our family structure advantages

while asking our parents for forgiveness

when we would disrespect them

verbally through ignorance, immaturity and carelessness.

I look back at the many times when

we as children played hide -n- seek

and the girls we had crushes on hid where we hid

and secretly gave us kisses on our cheeks.

We would immediately return the favor by buying

them their favorite candies and sweets

for these were the fun days that we referred

to as being "off the hook"

as we adopted, at no cost, slang terminology

in our everyday speech.

From dusk till dawn we played two-hand touch football

in the place of grass was glass that lay upon the streets

which inspired our athleticism to be full of rhythm

universally rather unique.

But there were times when our minds failed

to be agile but rather fragile and weak

which forced we the children to bond with

our childhood to its highest peak...

Understanding that our mission was then being guided to seek

outlets through our imaginations,

which would allow us to sacredly float

across Gods precious creek.

Sugar water kept us energetic so we stayed

faithful to buying quarter juices

however a lot of this energy was being wasted

as we physically fought rival youth

so through competing in sports we built common

ground as we formed many truces.

We played knock – knock zoom on neighbors doors and

when caught we offered no excuses

instead we would say sorry to pretend

and fifteen minutes later do it all again

using this experience to construct a wiser plan

in which we would be more elusive.

Amongst we the children, this excitement produced

an abundance of pure laughter

like games of cops and robbers where the slowest kid

was always the first to be captured...

Many of us didn't have the privilege of

having our own backyards

but we still designated patios and its surrounding

area as our meeting

spot to trade sports cards.

We even had fun hanging laundry on the windows protected

on the outside by steel bars

from where many spectators would watch us slap box

as we represented the hood as ghetto Olympians

when we tenaciously boxed and sparred...

These times delineated our building ideal knowledge of self

for we loved to shine like a star!

Some Saturdays we would load up in my father's station

wagon and go ocean fishing

for his purpose was to show us a world outside of the city

while grooming us to be young men and productive citizens

one of his prized ambitions.

During these fishing expeditions we were

able to see nature's true beauty at hand

it even inspired us upon returning home to

try our best to dispose of trash

no longer on the ground, but within its rightful place,

the dumpster or garbage can.

On the hottest of humid days, with no air conditioners,

in the windows we hoisted fans

as we sat and relaxed eating icies in attempt to

battle the heat's high demands.

I mean we were young kings and queens

able to accomplish all things

even though our castles were only built out of sand.

Our imaginations flourished boldly and colorful

like a thick box of crayons

we were the chosen generation of story tellers

who could stretch the truth

and one's perception wider than elastic rubber bands.

As children our eyes heard the trickery of

people trying to apply sales scams

so we would resiliently chase these

thieves away and alter their "get money" plans.

We would laugh our hearts away even when

the pursuit consisted of jumping fences

reminiscent of winter times when we would

throw snowballs at passing cars

while hiding in deep snow bank trenches.

Our actions were so playful that our growth seemed

inevitable to continue strengthening

we were so proud to be the one flower

in the garden that survived

through the winter, spring and fall without withering.

We would open up fire hydrants in the

summer and give passing cars a cool rinsing

dancing underneath these self-created waterfalls

provided us with much needed **H.O.P.E.**

of better days to come, as it relieved us

of so much negative tension.

As a child my eyes remember hearing the swiftness of the

horses we rode on at the carousel

as our vocal chords would expand with every twist and turn

as we would excitedly yell!

As a child my eyes remember hearing how

many people in society

viewed we the children as being frail

but only if they knew that we had the potential

to free the ship in the bottle

along with the heart to grant it freedom to set sail...

You see, as children we used rulers as sticks and created

drums out of empty paint pails

because we danced and sang to an original tune as we

creatively walked on our very own trail.

Admittedly, at times we were scared

to fail and even scared to excel

but we treated life like a picture waiting

to be hung and our futures were the hammer and nail...

As a child my eyes heard these whispers first as I began

to prepare for the challenge

of being a young educated black male.

It seems like yesterday when we would wake up at 6 o'clock

to watch Saturday morning cartoons

and race down the stairs to the kitchen to be the first

to get the biggest cereal spoons

it was like a circus of exquisite acrobats

huddled in our living room

as our eyes were glued to the television and our bodies

hugged the carpet tighter than the household sweeping broom.

Our sense of adventure blew up like balloons,

wide spread like heavy scented perfumes

as our self-esteem rocket launched and shined

amongst the stars as if it were the moon.

As a child my eyes heard the voices of our

ancestors when we wore African beads

and they also humorously reflect on when we would snatch

the patch off of other students Lee designed jeans...

Girls prepared to fight each other as they would

paint their "war" faces with Vaseline

to the extreme that their faces would look like

mirrors with a reflection so squeaky clean.

I mean, at the school bus stop we would

have the funniest rank sessions

so raw and uncut it was easily compared to graffiti,

an artistic expression in its own essence

without question, no matter what language

we were born predominately speaking

we all understood the voices of our childhood that spoke

to us during the week and weekends.

I remember Sunday school at church where we were taught

that the devil was our rival

as children we were more focused on winning candy

for quoting Bible verses via recital.

We had the most adorable smiles even

through the roughest of trials

because our hearts stretched wide as an odyssey,

extending for miles and miles...

Truthfully, we even threw torpedoes of rice at

newlyweds walking down church aisles

slyly balancing and maintaining a sincere

look of innocence all the while.

We cranked called the houses of anyone's phone

number we could remember and dial

because we were kids at heart who shined in the dark

with so much alluring style!

We made battleship a reality in the school

cafeteria by engaging in food fights

it was so comical when the cafeteria staff would

duck for cover and flick the lights

but then reality would set in when we would get punished

and grounded that very same night.

Oh, so very appreciative were we of our favorite toys who

were always accessible and willing to give advice.

During gym we would tuck and roll reminiscent of

the way we saw hustlers roll dice

so in a sense we gambled as we would bet

who could roll the fastest

the highest level of competition this act enticed.

As a child my eyes often heard the wind as

I began to wish I was a kite

so I could soar above my neighborhood

and view it from an aerial site

and look down upon children who teased chained dogs

regardless of fearing their bite

because although their eyes could hear their savage growl

they could never estimate the aggressiveness

of the dog's appetite.

However, I knew my appetite as I responded

to every birthday party and cookout invite

because free food always inspired a good mood

so there was nothing wrong with being right!

We would ride our bikes across town to a park

where we would go swimming

as those of us who looked older than we were

tried to attract the older women.

We were flattered as our hearts would

race like shooting stars in space

when in our direction we would see these women grinning

but of the course we knew the joke was on us

but to each other we would never admit it.

We all claimed to have known they were bluffing

our hearts from the very beginning

but we refused to shut off our adventurous light

for it was guaranteed never dimming

because to us children, losing was never an option

so we always believed in winning.

We were blessed and so refreshed like

the smell of just washed linen

curiosity of the world since newborns which served

as a sign of our growth transcending

for many of us were bred to always look ahead

towards the future and never the ending.

As if our wisdom teeth were tightly

secured and protected by braces

we were very thankful for the teachers whose

hearts and souls matched their smiling faces

for the knowledge they passed to us was

essential to our growth as they showed great patience

allowing us to see beyond the ghetto and discover the roots of

our world how its axis was global and beauteously spacious.

One teacher taught us the value of how

having flowers at home is a poem

when they are supported by vases

for each element depends on the other to

maintain a balance so gracious...

As a child my eyes remember exploring many perilous places

as I would dream of walking in the shoes of

Jack as he climbed the bean stalk venturing bravely into this

mysterious yet beautified enchanted oasis.

As a child I miss the days when we would trick the other kids

into thinking sour candy was tasteless

and how we would walk around town with our faces

looking down at our fat bright shoe laces...

Even the times when we would cry wolf

to avoid losing a game of marbles and jacks

just as we would cheat and memorize

the answer cards to trivial pursuit

and claim to be geniuses of worldwide facts

or when we would throw rocks at bee hives until

they declared war and decided to attack

as we would run our fastest like a strike of

lightning without daring to look back.

I remember the many times we would

stick half of our arm down the cereal box

to get the prize from inside but when asked if we retrieved it

we would lie being ever so cunning and

sly as a fox.

Just as rushing to get dressed in the

morning for school and putting on mismatched socks

and feeling like a clown with a frown

because our ankles were striped like candy

canes and color coated lollipops.

I remembered the personal lesson I learned when

my head turned in the barbershop

while I was in the chair and lost a big patch of hair

left to walk around with a bald spot!

As a child my eyes remember hearing arguments and broken

friendships over video games

they also remember hearing the ice cream trucks'

bells as we anxiously

broke open our piggy banks for change.

We fellas knew we were hot by the parts in our haircuts

that were designed like flames

and the girls were not to be outdone as they

waved their hips like the ocean

similar to cars swerving in and out of the fast lane.

These memories forever will be embedded in our minds

like jeans garnished by grass stains

because we lived for the moment of adventure evident by the

sugar rush that flowed freely and deep within our veins...

An excitement maintainable unlike the suspenders

that strapped my waist like a horses rein!

As children our eyes loved hearing

compliments from our parents

such as being great daughters and sons

thus, many of us responded by deciding not to use bullets

but instead water in our guns.

Just as Jolly Ranchers were the most

common perpetrator for colorizing our tongues

we made wave caps out of every pair

of our mothers' panty hose that had runs.

One outcome of being this creative led to

girls revealing their secret crushes

as our hearts judged this puppy love by counting all

of our sweethearts' many blushes

our hearts were so young and strung that we

credited cupid for his smooth clutches

on our lives because it instantly gave our

hearts the softest of rushes...

It should be noted that they were sugar-coated by cupids'

arrows which glazed them over like magical paint brushes.

As a child my eyes also tearfully remember

hearing many toilet flushes

from girls who thought my poetry was trash thus

they wouldn't give it thought for discussion

but I always kept a copy of this text – so easily I passed them

on to the next girl my heart was up to trusting!

After a long day of work mama would come

home and cook for the family

and still manage to find time to tuck me in

after we would say prayer together, an alleviating soft kiss on

my forehead would follow that she snuck in.

I mean the warmth of her affection was warmer

than my wool blanket – oh so comforting

I would fall sound asleep as my toy soldiers harmonized

peace by bringing their trumpets in.

In the morning I would awaken with cold in my eyes

but still could see my darling puppets grin

but I was humbled for I knew unfortunately

some children in my neighborhood

didn't sleep well at all and woke up suffering.

So I prayed to God and asked him to please

send them a hot bowl of chicken soup

for I believed it would heal their pain on route to walking

down the path of one trying to recoup.

I tried my best to believe that God's love would navigate

around their bodies like a hula hoop

Pop always said if we would believe then God would

oversee the success of we the youth group.

The very same youth who found a zany

truth in giving our friends wedgies

the same youth who loved to dispute with our parents

why we didn't need to eat veggies

we even got cute and offered replacements such

as the green frosted little Debbie's

we said resembled broccoli, lettuce and lima beans

which would provide our bodies with an

eating balance nice and steady.

Yeah, I will admit that our excuses, though funny,

were very ridiculous and petty

but one would have to admire our gift of gab

to string stories together spiced saucy like spaghetti.

As if we were on heaven's playground

sliding down a rainbow of blessings,

we were always ready

to ride the bus of life over the sky, tossing happiness to world,

in the form of sunny confetti!

As a child my eyes remember hearing free-style rap battles

as we engaged in verbal debates

with the sweat from our face roaring

at high speeds with no brakes

like high tides as we biked and raced.

My eyes remember hearing the rubber burn as

we chased the girls who were cruising on their roller skates

just as my eyes remember hearing mama walking up the stairs

with her belt in hand as our hearts trembled like earthquakes.

As children most of us didn't like adult drinks

but we loved coffee cakes

but as children when we didn't get our way our faces would

wrinkle like raisins with a true look of sour grapes.

For money we shoveled snow and discarded leaves with rakes

truth be told we were motivated by money and learned we

needed to develop work ethics for goodness sake.

As children we felt guilty for getting bad grades

which gave our parents heartaches

as they wouldn't always cry a river but rather

a decent sized lake.

We appreciated every meal provided as we beat dish

detergent to the punch by cleansing our plates

just as we loved to walk from school

and return home from third base.

At times our actions spoke louder but as children

we were still considered to be letters in

progress like that of the lower case

so often times we tried to balance our growth

by walking and talking at a slower pace.

I did say try but for some strange reason we thought

we all had the answers and lived in haste

often in our mouths was left a bitter taste.

Many adults saw through our charades like glass so

we tried to cover them with mental drapes

and avoid being verbally degraded by family

you know like being called a disgrace.

So we tried to polish our character like clean teeth,

consistently like tooth paste

but some pressures were unbearable like coming

in second during a race

some of our parents were competitive and believed

second place made us the first losers...

We justified their dissatisfaction by telling them we

were not heroes and we didn't wear capes

besides we knew the sunrise was our prize so

we didn't need a trophy or championship around our waist!

We didn't have tree houses in my neighborhood so we opted

instead to use abandoned buildings

the same ones our minds caught chills of being in but

our adventurous spirits refused yielding.

As children we really loved our neighborhood

for it was a place we never ever really felt concealed in

for there are memories of these apartment buildings that our

little sickly bodies were healed in.

Even the sandboxes where we fought and sometimes

blood from our noses was spilled in

and the infamous parking lot where a few hustlers from

our neighborhood were killed in

but our admiration of this environment

was never something prone to shielding

for even today we are still grateful for the many

experiences we gained as children...

Such as the days when we would put on an Oscar Award

performance and act like we were sick

running the thermometer beneath hot water

to assure that our plan would stick.

Admittedly, we would plot diligently, the night before as we

would edit our verbal script

for we wanted to be prepared to deliver this

plea to our parents in a gentle manner

versus looking overly cunning and sounding too slick.

On dirty mattresses we performed like acrobats

as we would bounce and flip

it seemed like our bodies were manufactured of pure

granite because at times we slipped

yet we would bounce right back up

re-energized like a fresh layer of bricks.

Our faces were stiff as mountains, sweat formed waterfalls

that would gradually drip

at the pace of a bull being rode frantically by the cowboy

while being continually whipped

but this only fed our enthusiasm an abundance

of adventure to continue to inflict.

During this time of **H.O.P.E.** it was okay

for young girls to play hop scotch

because they were universally protected and looked after

by the neighborhood block watch

which spread a feeling of freedom from constraint and harm

sweet as sugary pop tarts.

As a child my eyes remember hearing us "pop" on card board

boxes rather than pop car locks

we were the frame work of motor vehicles, with no brakes,

seat belts, license or shocks...

Timothy G. Green

As a child my eyes remember hearing my mother praying

during the winter and pollen season

for during this time my family was very prone to getting

sick and physically grieving.

I myself had a severe case of asthma as my chest would

often be found heavily wheezing

but my mother's timing perpetually seemed perfect as she

would arrive with medicine to rub

on my chest which assisted in strengthening

my lungs for better breathing.

As a child my eyes remember hearing my growing pains

during the time when I was teething

as I would anxiously eat my food, to test the strength

of my teeth, during my feeding.

My eyes also remember hearing Dr. Seuss rhyme

throughout all of my bed time readings

even during morning wake up, afternoon lunch and also over

eating snacks in the evening.

I remember how my sister's temper would flare stronger

than all of the 4th of July firecrackers

when I would get caught listening to her conversations

as I played the telephone hacker.

As a child it always amazed me how so many

people in society misunderstood

we the children and characterized us as bastards

they were unaware of the currency in our piggy banks

which proclaimed us as money stackers.

As children we were taught to set our goals high and aim

them towards the moon and stars

and thrust as much energy as possible when releasing

them hoping they'd travel beyond Mars.

As children many of us caught minor felonies such as getting

caught stealing from cookie jars

and many of us boys received suspended licenses from

recklessly driving match box cars.

Other children received warnings for playing too rough

with peers while on the monkey bars

as our parents hoped we learned lessons from these

incidents by our many physical scars.

As a child my friends and I could never manage

to run a lemonade booth

for we would voluntarily fall prey to the consistent

hunger of our own sweet tooth.

This was direct proof that we were so talented

and unique augmenting as youth

for although at times it came along as irrational,

we were still inclined to speak the truth.

At times we children were very untidy

and rightfully called home wreckers

so many of our parents began to discipline through

punishment which ruffled our feathers.

As a child my eyes remember hearing during dinner prayer

that we should forgive our debtors

and proceed to pursue happiness throughout all

of our current and future endeavors

for my father educated us to think strategic,

demonstrated during playing the game of checkers

teaching us that although we seemed to be pawns,

we could rise early like the break of dawn

as long as we continued to move forward through the

sunniest and stormiest of weathers.

Stormiest of weathers... playing outside in zero below

degrees until our hands were frost bitten

and frozen like icebergs while swelling our tiny

hands in our little wool mittens.

Angered parents blamed we the children even though

someone was in charge of baby sitting

we were young at age and full of energy so we rebelled

choosing to portray our steadfast love for adventure,

so to our baby sitters we refused to listen.

Truthfully, when I recited my poetry I could

sense the honor of those witnessing

so I tried my very best to give a presentation

that my audience would find interesting

because As a child my eyes remember hearing

gentle sentiments of the crowd whispering

keep on, keep on, keep on, keep on...

Many girls and boys learned the foundation of

responsibility through completing chores

in which some of us got paid and saved our money

where others had their minds made up and headed

directly to the stores.

Coming home to the television, with the hanger antenna,

was a moment we children adored

Timothy G. Green

as we sat in front of the television on the floor and turned

the channels manually to explore.

My eyes remember hearing momma scream from the kitchen

as I would pretend to ignore

but before she knew it, my movement was very fluid,

and with trash bags in my hands I would

be out the front door.

As children, growing up in our neighborhood,

we weren't ashamed to be poor

because we could rest assured in a manner mature,

that our parents would do everything possible to make

sure our stomachs would never roar.

You see, there were many days that

we children were overwhelmed in elation

portraying indication that beneath God's sky

we could all engage in united celebration.

Without hesitation, we were all thankful that in heaven

an abundance of cherubs were waiting

which enlightened the doves from above to release

peace via **Happiness Of Prayers Embracing!**

I mean, we the children have physical scars to reflect upon

thus one would never know

how much this pain, even today, still hurts,

but knowing that many of us survived this attrition

has proved to be very therapeutic

so in this form - our soul's continue to be nursed

for this inspired our sense of curiosity, like breast milk,

it always quenched our thirst.

So many times we heard our parents speaking

of paying so much homage

that mournfully we would find them

asking God to be reimbursed,

they often felt like the **P.A.I.N.** embracing our young

generation was surely a sign of us being cursed.

Especially when many of us unfortunately

had to ride to the cemetery,

pine boxed in a hearse

for we were prize fighters who fought everyday of our lives

because survival was the purse.

Yet, As a child I remember hearing stories of

how our struggle was scripted and written

by God and his and beloved angels verse by precious verse

so you see, it could have been scripted and written

by Satan and his demons, in a nutshell, a whole lot worse.

However, we were chosen to overcome this adversity

and represent the strength of **H.O.P.E.**

Thus, humbly I speak of and record these

statutes which **As a child my eyes heard it first....**

E.Y.E.G.

Eventually Young Eyes Sing

flesh wounds

When impregnated hate penetrated her soul
helplessly her children were breast fed agony
as she opted to sale her body not for money
but for a glimpse of what she claimed to be love

Daddy was a color blind walking zombie
artistically drawn to white lines
urine scented the apartment carpet to carpet
debris used for pillows to comfort weary heads
no lights for visual as shadows reigned supreme
roaches roamed freely and claimed their territory
in this mystified Rubik's Cube

leaky faucets played the blues for daily entertainment
as growling stomachs covered the bass tone
damned like a torn hymnal of hunger paining
chap lips mumbled sweet nothings
wisdom teeth slowly decaying
sleep disturbed by vomit choking lungs
with a mission to kill
being a firsthand witness as child

Eventually Young Eyes Sing
Timothy G. Green

Enter Narrator: Timothy G. Green

Scene location for every act: Abandoned building rooftop

Act 1

<u>Something never held can never be lost: Love</u>

As a child my eyes heard many stories from the roof of this abandoned building. One of them came from the apartment building just to the left of this building. A loud noise was heard, so naturally my childlike instincts set in as I went to explore the scene. At the time, judging from the size of their living room window, it looked like a soap opera on a big screen television. There was a woman who looked shaken as she argued with a man. He was pacing the room back and forth with a very noticeable stagger. Judging by the vomit on his shirt and the waterfall of sweat pouring from his head I could tell that he was drunk. Nervously I watched as this man backed into a china cabinet and altered its balance. Unfortunately, most of the china was destroyed as they fragmented upon landing on the surface of the floor. Somberly, they shattered like contorted happy memories. Suddenly, the woman's irritation must have grown as she furiously began breaking the remaining china at will. She screamed,

"I have spent the last eight years going through this and I've had enough."

Boldly she began pointing towards the door, which served as a gesture for her wanting him to leave. His response was simple. A motioning head shake of "no" followed by ridiculing laughter. The man then pumped his fist at her in a threatening manner. His walk was slow but focused as he moved towards the woman. With urgency her eyes roamed, assessing the room. Calmly she knelt to the floor and picked up a piece of broken china. Just as the man got within striking distance with a raised hand, my eyes could hear the woman tighten her grip on the rigid piece of china. This was evident from the blood that rapidly released from her palm. All of a sudden both of their heads simultaneously turned towards a moving shadow. From this shadow a young boy emerged. His face was pale and his expression was terrified. The act that then followed served the scene as the beginning of the end for this child.

In no specific order the woman and the man begin bombarding this child with profanities and insults. My eyes remember hearing the woman make references of how she hates the child for having such a strong physical resemblance to his father. My eyes remember hearing the man tell the child of a malicious regret; wishing the child was never born. As if the young boy and I were communicating telepathically, his body turned and he ran towards his room as my feet moved as well on the rooftop in pursuit of him. I proceeded to the stairwell that would exit me from the building top.

I remember lying in bed that night crying nonstop. My mind raced at a restless pace, wondering the fate of the young boy. Two days later the local newspaper had the face of the young boy on its front page. He was found dead in his bedroom with both of his wrists slit. I know in my heart that the young boy must have had no more tolerance for his parents after many years of **P**ain, **A**gony, **I**gnorance and **N**eglect. His aspirations of seeing the **H**appiness **O**f **P**rayers **E**mbracing weren't seen at his home on earth, thus he figured to take a short cut to a home awaiting him in Heaven. Sadly, this was his escape route... Whether we as adults understand the mental rhythm and lyrics of our youth or not, they will continue to portray every time that **Eventually Young Eyes Sing**!

Act 2

<u>Heroin or Heroine: Shades of deceit...</u>

From this viewpoint on the rooftop we can see a stunning mural with lit candles bordering it. Highlighting the mural is the face of one of God's beloved Angels. Isn't she so beautiful? Sadly, deep within the sparkle of her eyes dwells a horrid story of how her innocence was prematurely deemed guilty, due to a biased judge during the myriad of trials she experienced during her short life. Even though she passed away many yesterdays ago she is still a part of today and shall continue to be loved tomorrow as well. Allow my mind and eyes to narrate her dramatic story and paint a verbal collage for you.

She was a four year honor roll student who could have easily built skyscrapers with the tons of letters she received daily from every major university across the United States. At school her smile was embedded within the hallways and classrooms, bringing forth a scintillating energy. That is why the day she was found weeping in study hall was noted as strange. As she read a poem from the school newspaper titled, "The Spark of My Life," her tears comprised its print as if they were written with it. The poem was written by a fellow student who expressed his undying love for his mother. Her hand was sweating from her tight clutch of the locket which draped from her neck and lay centered between her breasts. As if this locket was the *Scarlet Letter* she tore it from her neck as if its weight held significant mental strain on her life. Many of her classmates knew within this locket was a picture of her mother. Sorrowfully, she was known around town as a prostitute.

With cloudy eyes she began to converse with the locket in whispers that were chillingly low and mystical. The volume of her whispers began to rise with a paramount of intensity. In fact, the whispers grew into a sullen spoken word for all to hear.

"Mother, why don't you love me? When you were pregnant with me hate must have penetrated deep into your soul. I must have been breast fed your agony as a child and now I experience this agony emotionally, knowing that you sale your body for money. Is that love mother? Is it?! You're fully capable of working but you've chosen to surrender your body and remain dependent on your state checks. Your choice mother! Yours!

Not even the lingering urine scent throughout our apartment smells as putrid as your ignorance. You're too busy lusting after love from men for money to see that my tear drops leak daily in concert with the rusty faucet in our kitchen. My growling stomach can't even be heard let alone my abundant pleas to you. You're my mother! I care not about people's opinions; I'm starving for just one girl's night out. Instead, it's always mom's night out, selling her soul. To think of how hard I have worked to maintain; to remain an honor roll student and you have yet to acknowledge this accomplishment. I'm sick of IT! I'll find another way to make you proud mommy, this I promise!"

As if the rule of silence wasn't being administered, it immediately made its presence felt in the study hall. The hearts and lungs of the students and faculty must have collapsed, for everyone was speechless from hearing her words of affliction.

What followed a few weeks later was the uncharacteristic absence of this love-stricken honor roll student for the remainder of the semester. Classmates and teachers alike wore unbearable looks on their faces of dispirited concern. Phone calls home were found ineffective because the phone was out of service. Home visits weren't effective either as neighbors told school staff that the family was evicted.

Then one morning the high school principal called for an emergency school gathering in the auditorium. With a hoarse voice and dampened eyes he informed his students and school faculty that their beloved honor roll student had been murdered over the weekend. His request of a moment of silence was mournfully ignored as souls and hearts wept appalled as a collective.

You see, the soul of this young girl was lost in a state of chagrin. She decided to taste this "realm" of her mother's happiness by indulging in it herself. Thus, she decided to parade the streets and sell her body too in hopes that this would please and garner the attention of her mother. Unfortunately, she had no knowledge that her mother was in debt with some local drug dealers. Upon seeing her, these drug dealers stood bewildered by her flawless resemblance to her mother. They figured they would send a message to her mother by raping and torturing her. Heroically she must have fought back, as police reports documented traces of blood from her assailants having been found beneath her finger tips. However, the morose fact remains that she was murdered.

Eventually **Young Eyes Sing** though, for the sparkled highlights in her eyes on the mural seem as if they are still seeking acceptance and love from her mother whom still can be found canvassing the city streets as a prostitute...

Act 3

Under the influence and soon the Earth

Blocks down what do you see? Exactly! Another package store… What you and I can't see from this building top is the number of package stores not only surrounding neighborhoods but established within them too. Listen closely, because I say all that to say this. The very same liquor that is poured out in tribute to fallen angels is the very same liquor that I've seen travel deep within the hearts of men and nauseate their conscience. It's only fitting that I use pieces of these broken liquor bottles on this building rooftop to reflect upon, while narrating this next story.

In this particular family a father chose to make his home his personal package store. Whoever opened the refrigerator had to reach around an array of different alcoholic beverages in order to reach the milk carton or even a stick of butter. Even the freezer fell into this adventure as shot glasses gated ice trays, frozen waffles and gallons of ice cream. The signature aroma of alcohol scented this father daily like cologne. His two children, one boy and one girl, declined to have their friends visit because of the potential embarrassment he would cause. Instead, they opted to use the telephone when speaking to their friends. Even then their fathers irritating presence was felt as his emotional breakdowns led to loud verbal tirades and emotional outbursts. This ultimately portrayed the dominant reign of the alcohol within his body.

The children often wished they could be excused from participating in family dinner. They would help their mother prepare the table for serving,

113

which was found pre-polished many times from spilled liquor. Upon finishing, their father would have already consumed four cans of beer. Their mother, whom seemed to barricade his behaviors from her mind, would then proceed to politely ask the children about their experiences at school for that day. The children, however, were always were very hesitant to answer. Every time the children would announce an accomplishment it seemed as if a mental recourse would occur in their father's mind. His mind seemed to revert back to being in a bar atmosphere as he would toast his beer bottle against his children's Styrofoam or glass cups while releasing a very quaint yet drunken laugh. Although his bloodshot eyes disguised his distress, it was very evident that time would reveal his internal misery.

The children never understood why momma continued to stand by this man. Her skin appeared to be like concrete when he would verbally abuse her. Yet, it swiftly became a destitute canvas in the form of being colorized dark black and blue when he would physically assault her. Regardless of what the children saw as overwhelming evidence and reason to leave him, their mother did not. He was her high school love and she refused to exit him from her life. She relied in **H.O.P.E.** that he would change yet she grew accustomed to his behaviors and had her heart set on him.

Unfortunately, a few years later the wedding vow "until death do us part" was enforced by his hands, as she would sadly die from excessive head trauma. Upon her death there was insufficient evidence to convict him of murder. Yet, death lurked closely in his shadow and found the opportunity to greet the father by the use of his own hands too. A few years later he was killed instantly, while fleeing from the authorities, by crashing into two parked cars. His autopsy report indicated that his body was intoxicated four times over the drinking limit.

The spirit of karma followed and sculpted his daughter's life as well. She ended up marrying an abusive husband who was an alcoholic. She gave birth to their first child alone, as her husband was being held in jail at the time for domestic abuse. You see, she flirted with ideas of divorcing him yet she removed a restraining order she had filed against him. She had a false sense of love and loyalty from the example that her mother had set. Since his release from prison he has continued to assault her and even threatened her on the premises of her work site. By way of her husband's instruction she stopped talking to her brother and other family members as well. She moved with him out of state and never told her family of her location nor updated them with a current phone number to reach her.

Act 4

<u>Every flower must grow through the dirt</u>

Word has gotten out that the city plans to finally destroy this abandoned building. What they plan to put in its place is still unknown but nonetheless this may be my last reflection from this rooftop. Judging from the speed of the winds draft I can tell that heavy rain is on the way. I'm willing to bet that no matter how great its downpour, there's no way possible that it can compare to the excruciating precipitation that my soul is getting set to release… Let your E.Y.E.S. listen closely, to the deep truth of me, the narrator, Timothy G. Green.

"Though no one can go back and make a brand new start, anyone can start from now and make a brand new ending."

Author Unknown

Depression's diet calls for one to chew on a book of matches

while dejectedly staring and feasting

on your life's most painful moments in fragments

happiness seemed to be mystified

my soul deemed to be hypnotized

within the matrix of reality and illusion headlining

with fear as the face of these theatrics

so why not gargle with gasoline in hopes to

vomit (release) my heart in ashes?

Unjustly touched by my doctor in a cowardly

act of betrayal and broken innocence

I grew a fiery hatred for this once trusted hypocrite

for years my mind would be tortured by the

vocal chords of this perverted ventriloquist

who violently ruptured my souls penmanship

with no expressed permission of censorship;

to any part of my life's story…

My self confidence then went on a downward spiral

and formed into a distorted prism

my thoughts wandered liked a string-less guitar

asthmatic in search of breath through a joyful rhythm

as my intuition was in a famine state

starving for peace of mind found directly in wisdom.

From the horrid stench of these shadows

there seemed to be no escape

my eyes would close for hours

but my E.Y.E.S. would remain open and fully awake

frosty tears turn the mountains

on my cheeks into a frozen lake,

as breath from my mouth releases deformed snowflakes

meaning anger immaturely released to ALL

whom I encounter with the sole intent of heartbreak;

prematurely I even ran away from He

who promised to never leave nor forsake.

Depression rented a space in my mind

without even signing a lease

along with a handful of peers and family members

teasing me often for being overweight and obese.

I was even scared to smile because of the gap

that resides between my top two teeth,

continuously told by elders and teachers to rise

above the negative tide

but I always found my emotions drowning beneath,

as the spirit of "woe is me" continued

crowning me with me grief…

Being labeled as the "fat kid"

often my eyes wept

loneliness had me counting the stretch marks on my biceps,

"try and fail or fail to try" to survive

I openly began to embrace this concept,

luckily I was gifted in playing basketball

which garnered high praise from my peers

with honor and a sense of respect.

I began entering poetry contests

which was splendid indeed

as I verbally massaged the minds of readers

and audiences by making my pen bleed

recognition birthed a flame – yet I tamed

a grin of greed

remembering the oath of

"never compromising my character"

to my pen and notebook I pledged this creed…

Forever grateful for the breakthrough discovery

of being "expressively" gifted

wretchedly ashamed of my lack of academic

focus and effort

in which my high grades swiftly drifted

with the promotion of my Father to heaven

my attitude and perspective on life shifted

unbalanced in every area

like an overflow of maple syrup on biscuits

Momma's words of encouragement kept me uplifted

yet poor decision making had me act as the lookout

as a few of my friends shoplifted

my mind state was unstable with uncertainty

like that of an infant

as I never fit in with the crowd

but stood out with the misfits.

Within myself I had to set aside the hatred

so I began to slowly but surely

speak life within myself

whispering "Tim, you're going to make it!"

Funny because although I was an aspiring young novelist

I wrote the most baffling and disorganized letters

to local and highly esteemed colleges

telling tales of heartbreak and broken promises

innocently as I was looking for their sympathy.

Looking back at being the youngest child

at times I was excessively spoiled

I got away with many ill behaviors that

that made my siblings blood boil

but believe it or not I too received discipline

that grew deep within my hearts soil

once I even planned to wrap

my buttocks with aluminum foil...

Trust me I know — I know

stupidity at his finest that didn't make sense

because my parents were extremely heavy handed

able to penetrate justice through any defense...

blessed to learn budgeting at an early age

through shopping by way of consignment

to hustle through the struggle kept my mind in alignment

with understanding the value system of currency

which could alter at any moment

challenging one to adjust with its climate

in truth the motto of stretching a penny

I solemnly swear my father had to design it

or he had a hidden treasure chest

buried in our backyard by way of solitary confinement.

Sibling feuds over who ate someone's leftover food

or dominating the house telephone

purposely being spiteful and verbally rude

privacy didn't fully exist in our bedrooms

as we would often intrude

leading to warfare through arguments

and placing mom in the foulest of moods.

But the love we shared broke every cord of friction

Saturday cartoons assisted in destroying all negative tension

not to mention

humor was a welcomed addiction

as laughter rightfully deployed our pride to suspension.

I remember as teenagers when my boys and I

would rock Members Only jackets

mine was so tight that it poked holes in my

chest like a tennis racket

I also remember the times that we would be

on the phone for hours ranking;

it would get real personal

but we would quickly bury the hatchet.

Disappointed that As A Child I believed

the myth of friendships being endless

I was overly hurt by

this false tense of eternity

when friendships ended from things I believed were senseless

lovingly I unlocked my heart;

foolishly I left it defenseless.

In transparency these were my imperfections

I was just a young man in search of self

let alone a path to travel with clear direction.

I was in a rush to prematurely birth dreams

tormented every time a childhood friend was buried

hearing the shrieking cries of the earth scream

no matter how obvious my talent would seem

being young and overweight

distorted my focus severely on life's balance beam…

Yet and still I have no regrets

on my adventurous childhood journey

in which I eventually learned not to "fit in"

because loving thyself is the greatest gift

for one to feel worthy

dreamed of having my name on the back

of a professional sports team jersey

but if I didn't accept myself

then within my own soul I was committing burglary…

As A Child so many people were hard on me

so to protect myself I stayed

on the defense like an attorney

I handed people the match (light) to my heart

and some used it to burn me

through broken promises in the form of emotional perjury

countless sleepless nights

in ominous need of open heart surgery…

Nervously, I followed momma's advice

to still live earnestly

and exert wisdom to no longer

allow my peers to refurnish me.

The same mouth that was slicker than grease

was the very same mouth that prayed to God

consistently – requesting a blessing of peace

in losing patience to wait

I gained weight in the form of obese

on and off my faith would fold like a crease

until I grew strong enough to fight the hurt and release;

through writing – armed with my pencil I was a Titan

my words were inviting

some poems were dark but others were written to enlighten…

I purposely lit papers on fire

I called it verbal arson

Learned to love myself despite being teased

for having dark skin

learned to pray and protect my heart

from allowing fiery darts in

only to find that my so called friends

were really unknown enemies and marksmen…

Experience taught me that life was a game of inches

to watch the words of man

because the tongue was powerfully cunning and convincing

between happiness and sorrow

there was a fine line of distinction

that if I didn't learn to love myself

then with depression and transgression

my mind would be imprisoned.

Reflecting on senior year

how I graduated from summer school

I felt lower than the Earth's surface

as my peers called me a dumber fool

I took it personal because back then

at various times

I operated with the mentality of younger fuel

until I matured and utilized their insults

as a hunger tool

and today my life is tremendously blessed

by the grace of God something WONDERFUL;

Only because as A Child My Eyes Heard It First!

1 Corinthians 13:11 New Living Translation

"When I was a child, I spoke and thought and reasoned as a child.

But when I grew up, I put away childish things."

About the Author

Timothy G. Green is an educator at heart. Aside from being a Program Coordinator, he also provides leadership workshops via poetry and motivational speaking to local community based organizations.

Having released **Roses are Read: Love lost or found** this year along with the Roses Are Read clothing imprint, this is his second book to be published through INKaissance Books: **As A Child My Eyes Heard It First: 2ⁿᵈ Edition**. He looks to build upon their success with this "**Poetic Novel**" as well. The 3ʳᵈ book slated to be released later this year/early 2020 from INKaissance Books is: **Innocence In A Sense**.

He is a Christian and blessed husband to a beautiful wife and honored to be a father of a 13 year old daughter and a 6 year old son. He is also the proud founder of INKaissance. He continues to seek innovative ways to assist the Hartford community with leadership, social, and educational opportunities. Being recognized as a servant leader is a privilege that he doesn't underestimate nor under value.

Connect with Timothy G. Green.

> e-mail: inkaissance@gmail.com
>
> Facebook: Timothy G. Green
>
> Instagram: timothy_inkaissance_green